Field Notes
in Contemporary Literature

C. J. Sage

Dream Horse Press
California

Other books by C. J. Sage:

Let's Not Sleep
And We The Creatures
Odyssea

.

Dream Horse Press
California

Library of Congress Cataloging-in-Publication Data:

p.   cm

ISBN 0-9-777182-9-8
1. Poetry

10 9 8 7 6 5 4 3 2 1

First Edition

Poetry

C. J. Sage

Sonnet for Carryhouse and Keeper

I met a man who'd kept a snail as pet
beneath a cold stone house which held no wife;
too dank it was for even cats to thrive.
Inside an old fish tank his snail friend slept.

The man's round back was proof he'd not forget
to spend good time in keeping things alive
between his care-filled self and his shelled bride.
All day he'd curve around her as she crept

among the leafy shadows of his hands;
he'd trace her pearl-string trails with his fingers,
his breath would set small clouds into her glass.

The day he set her free she took one half
a day to slip into good-bye; she lingered
in the lovegrass, like the lovelorn, said this man.

Content questions:
*1. Which claims are the speaker's and which are the man's? Why is it important
to consider the difference?*
*2. Why does the poet choose a snail instead of a dog or a cat? Why a snail instead of,
say, a parrot or a lovebird? How does the answer to these questions help illuminate
the message of the poem?*
3. In what ways do people often behave similarly to the man in the poem?

Form questions:
*1. Traditionally, part of being a sonnet is having a rhyme scheme. Does this
poem rhyme?*
2. Sonnets often contain a volta—a turn or shift. Does this one?

C. J. Sage

How to Keep a Setter

Understand that attraction
to the birds is only natural.

He might be trained to sway
from posturing and pointing,

but don't demand prostration
of the face. A high-held mask of pride
helps him become your champion.

Don't just pat his head — stroke
the golden apple of his throat.

On balmy evening walks, don't hurry.
Let him nose the honeyed air, the grass.
Maybe take a tumble in it with him.

When he comes to your sweet call,
remember you aren't the only creature
singing. Applaud the concentration.

For some it's a question of chemistry.
For others, a matter of best-friendship.

And oh, what people do for such

companions. Learn to love the dirt

or if you love it learn to show it.

Learn to love the killer instinct,

and the dumbness that's the basis

of loyalty. He wears your leash

and prances happily at your side.

You lead sometimes, sometimes he.

Content questions:
1. This is a didactic poem. To whom is the speaker giving instructions?
2. A setter is a type of dog. Is there anything in the poem that we do not typically associate with dogs?
3. In stanza six, the speaker associates "singing" with the addressee. Comparing that fact with an earlier stanza, what might we infer about the addressee? Is s/he similar to any other thing in the poem?

Form questions:
1. Explain how the line break at the end of line one might work to help put forth the meaning of the poem. Are there other line breaks that do the same thing?
2. Looking for connotation, can we identify diction that helps to hint at the poem's meaning?

C. J. Sage

The Dark Pelican

Her nest is crude (though on the shore it rests,
it rests on stone). Her nest: a twiggy hole, the crib
from which she watches water as it climbs and crests

the seawall. Between those hard and arching ribs
of rock around her home she spans her wings —
and on the foggy screen of saltspray how they scribble!

Her neck a spliny thread stretched and swinging,
back she throws her head to throat the little fish
she'd kept in close, the fish she'd saved for evening.

O just a swish of bony flesh against the falling dish

of sunset, she has found her food the hard way;
she has cast herself head-first into her wishes

while in their circles lighter sisters sway
and wait together — they watch and drive the catch,
they snatch it up in turns; like rose-tint dawn their days

are easy. But the one who works alone must patch
together what she can. (For friends there is no match.)

Suggestions:
*Sometimes, a little research will help us understand a poem. Look up the hunting
behavior of white pelicans versus brown pelicans.*

C. J. Sage

The San Simeon Zebras

Like many,
they are out of place:

stolen and content.

So wild in expressing
their timidity, they are wholly

hidden; their hides are more
dizzying than their presence:

dark and lightness,

confused as to the meaning
of their being
here, as they are.

— What an invitation!—
that wire-slatted hillside. —

Largely overwhelming
as the masses

of an outcast, homeless people.

—Lost so completely
everyone is, in passing, interested.

C. J. Sage

Field Notes

A stealthy pride of lions
stalks the one who went too far
alone; about his grazing business

the buffalo moves on
but all the while looking back,
doe-eyed, behind himself.

Following his measured pace
his predators are slow and patient.
They hide in the savanna grass

and oh how low they crouch.
How they slide, as if battle
trained, on their bellies.

And when they come upon him
he doesn't seem surprised, though
he hoofs the ground and bellows,

though he shakes his head
side to side when a young one
stows its claws into his rump.

Another pounces, rides his back,
another on his hind legs
takes him down. Does he know

it yet—his time is over? Denied

all dignity, their teeth inside his back,
he throws them off, he fights

his way into a nearby swamp
to lie and catch his breath, to wait.
Another stroke of hope: the herd

from which he'd strayed lines up
on the horizon, chides the cats
to back them off. The hunters go

a distance, and when they do
one buffalo strides into the water
to lick the victim's flesh wounds,

she kisses them—awhile.
The herd, with thrashing horns and spirit,
heroic for a moment, decides now,

suddenly, we don't know why,
to retreat. They leave him in the swamp:
food for the determined—stupefied.

Content questions:
1. *Why is the buffalo "stupefied"?*
2. *Does the poem present a moral?*

Form questions:
1. *Is this a free verse poem?*
2. *Can we locate any sort of rhyme pattern?*
3. *In stanza 12, why is the word "awhile" set off with the emdash? Would there be a different meaning if there were nothing but a space between "them" and "awhile"?*

Bob Hicok

Who'll Say Dugong When the Dugong's Gone?

Kiss a mermaid while you can.
They're twelve feet long
and have bones thick as ivory.

The myth-conception began
when sailors, rummed or simply
craving beauty, confused

the sixteen-hundred-pound dugong
for a glistening woman in fins.
Because the dugong's almost

extinct, mermaids will soon
abandon our stories. Already
we don't quote the Cyclops

or ask the Minotaur to drinks.
Remember this rule
from economics: less is less

interesting. Subtract
the dugong with its one hair
per square inch from Kupang

Bay and Arakan Reef, take
the snow leopard and the snow
itself and soon we'll have Cleveland

from here to the Antilles.

The dugong swims and eats and makes
dugongs, it's a shadow

within the shadow of the sea
and not us, reason enough
for it to live. Sometimes

I think the bulldozer's how we say
that only the world we make
is real. There are nights

I try to grow a beard & hook,
try to let stars burn a map
on the inside of my skull

as I rise and fall on the breath
of water, I'm the kind
of sailor who'll walk the plank.

On my way down I want to see
that whiskered face, not human
but calm, a mammal happy

to be where it happens to be,
which is joy and something
you'd never say about us.

Content question:
Why is the dugong's "one hair / per square inch" important to the poem?

Form question:
Of all the things to which one might compare a dugong's bones, why does the poet choose ivory?

W. S. Merwin

Plea for a Captive

Woman with the caught fox

By the scruff, you can drop your hopes:

It will not tame though you prove kind,

Though you entice it with fat ducks

Patiently to your fingertips

And in dulcet love enclose it

Do not suppose it will turn friend,

Dog your heels, sleep at your feet,

Be happy in the house,

           No,

It will only trot to and fro,

To and fro, with vacant eye,

Neither will its pelt improve

Nor its disposition, twisting

The raw song of its debasement

Through the long nights, and in your love,

In your delicate meats tasting

Nothing but its own decay

(As at first hand I have learned)

           Oh

Kill it at once or let it go.

Ted Kooser

Coyotes

My pup steps to the edge

of the light from our porch

and barks her obbligato

into the huge auditorium

of the winter night. Out there,

critics with yellow eyes,

dressed in snow-sparkled furs,

turn to each other and, without

a sound, curl up their lips.

Questions:
1. In "Plea for a Captive," what is the one line that stands out as being different from the rest, and how might it help us interpret the poem?
2. The pup in "Coyotes" "barks her obbligato." What is an obbligato, and what would cause one to "bark" it?
3. What are the connotations of "yellow"? Of 'stepping to the edge'?

Jeffrey Skinner

The Climbers

Poor men. On either side a green shield
angled against their ascent. The summit then
snagged in cloud. Or, the false drama
of clarity, senses free of obstruction —

Look, everyone, everywhere I turn, I see!
But poor Jesus had God's ear, curled
inside, and no need of height to hear, static-
free. He descended into desert.

Poor men. They climb like a column
of ants, lugging heartache on their backs
as if it were food. They set up camp
and a few freeze, a few return. But the danger

is minimal. Most stumble down,
throw knapsacks in the trunk, drive home —
What air, what views! Poor men. Poor Jesus,
blinking away the sun with his endless *No.*

Content questions:
1. *Elaborate how these climbers are like ants.*
2. *Consider how heartache might be like food.*

Form question:
1. *Identify any refrains in this poem and consider how they help bring focus to the poem's meaning.*

David Wagoner

Peacock Display

He approaches her, trailing his whole fortune,
Perfectly cocksure, and suddenly spreads
The huge fan of his tail for her amazement.

Each turquoise and purple, black-horned, walleyed quill
Comes quivering forward, an amphitheatric shell
For his most fortunate audience: her alone.

He plumes himself. He shakes his brassily gold
Wings and rump in a dance, lifting his claws
Stiff-legged under the great bulge of his breast.

And she strolls calmly away, pecking and pausing,
Not watching him, astonished to discover
All these seeds spread just for her in the dirt.

Question:
Why does a "peacock" work so well as the hero of this poem?

Wesley McNair

The Puppy

From down the road, starting up
and stopping once more, the sound
of a puppy on a chain who has not yet
discovered he will spend his life there.
Foolish dog, to forget where he is
and wander until he feels the collar
close fast around his throat, then cry
all over again about the little space
in which he finds himself. Soon,
when there is no grass left in it
and he understands it is all he has,
he will snarl and bark whenever
he senses a threat to it.
Who would believe this small
sorrow could lead to such fury
no one would ever come near him?

To consider:
Have you ever seen a puppy on a chain?

Natural Enemies

All day the owl is dreaming of a crow, dreaming
of a crow, dreaming of a crow and his war caw
rushing through the pines, and the owl opens
her mouth as if to say wait, wait until nightfall,
until nightfall when the crow's own blackness
is not enough to hide him from her keen eyes.

All night the crow is dreaming of an owl, dreaming
of an owl, dreaming of an owl and battle screech
so close it could run through his dark body and sever
his spine. His mouth moves in silence: wait, wait
until daybreak when the owl's gray camouflage
cannot protect her from the murders of crows.

In twilight the owl and crow are praying to live, praying
to live, praying to live the long hours of hunting. They do
not fly nor tempt the other into the unowned time
and orange territory of conflicted light. They bide, bide
in their pine churches with their psalms to a god
who would favor their feathers over the other's.

Content questions:
1. *How do we know that the poem is about more than owls and crows?*
2. *Why are owls and crows used for the poem's metaphor?*

Form questions:
1. *What do the refrains do for the poem?*
2. *Are there any other patterns in the poem?*

J. P. Dancing Bear

West Nile

The birds began to rust,

brown dust, life sparking away.

Starting with one dropped note

like an autumn leaf.

I thought if I buried them,

then a flock might rise up,

come back Lazuren, Orphic,

a darker but deeper beauty.

With tunes to conjure the thinking

mind to ice cliffs eroding,

forests blackening,

little harbinger songs—

terrible angelic lurching

dirges that almost fumed

in choking carbon rage.

But nothing comes

so splendidly announced.

The messengers sit Cassandran

in their cells, listening as the first

ship plagues its soldiers onto shore.

Questions:
1. *The author has said that this poem is "ecopolitical." Do you agree? Why or why not?*

2. *What interpretive approaches would be most helpful to understanding the poem?*

Robin Behn

Red and Black Days

Sometimes they would gather at the table,

the woman and the boy and the man

whose cheer lately had come to stay

along with the royal possibilities

a day of checkers afforded.

Crown me! the boy would say.

Kings and kings and kings.

The boy moved them forward

and back in space and time,

and sideways, and snake-like, and

like hopscotch and gazelles.

A little red fiefdom of his own design

with a side street for the underlings

to dwell in. The pauper population

growing, cheering! Tossing up

their thin black caps!

Questions:
1. Is there a refrain here? If so, how does it work?
2. What interpretive approaches would be most useful to understanding the poem?

Robin Behn

Interlude: Still Still

Inside the hole, where it's yellow,

the boy has dropped a quarter

so that the guitar rattles

when he shakes it by the neck.

Knocks, scrapes, scars.

So this is what music is.

The wooden body is no longer

bigger than his body.

The strings, which, when

he strums them,

go on forever are forever

wound around small pegs

shaped like the big ones

they wrap the ropes around,

there being an absence of

able-bodied mourners

to lower, with the softer machines

of their bodies, the coffin down.

It was a cold day.

The boy had not been born yet,

but stood among us

warm in his round place.

Then, from the distance,

the bagpiper who'd been found

in the yellow pages

extracted the horizon note

like a red needle from the sky.

And so it was not with nothing

human our friend was lowered.

This is what music is.

But how did it sound to the boy,

the bladder of cries squeezed

through the slit throat

when there had not been anything

yet to cry about?
The solace of music is

not that we recognize it.
It is that the hearing
comes from before and is wound

around after. Between,
our bad singing a stranger
dozed, then bulldozed, too.

At home, in its case, the guitar
was hunkered inside the dark
into which music goes,

and the more particular dark
from which music comes
was inside of it.

The sound hole swallowed and passed back
buckets of silence
until the inner and outer dark

had the same yellow smell.

This, while the song the boy

would pay for waited, still still.

Jennifer Michael Hecht

September

Tonight there must be people who are getting what they want.
I let my oars fall into the water.
Good for them. Good for them, getting what they want.

The night is so still that I forget to breathe.
The dark air is getting colder. Birds are leaving.

Tonight there are people getting just what they need.

The air is so still that it seems to stop my heart.
I remember you in a black and white photograph
taken this time of some year. You were leaning against
a half-shed tree, standing in the leaves the tree had lost.

When I finally exhale it takes forever to be over.

Tonight, there are people who are so happy,
that they have forgotten to worry about tomorrow.

Somewhere, people have entirely forgotten about tomorrow.
My hand trails in the water.
I should not have dropped those oars. Such a soft wind.

Questions:
1. Identify the patterns in this poem.
2. Is there anything in the poem that can be taken two opposite ways?

Eric Rawson

A Leopard Hanging in a Tree

A leopard hanging in a tree:
Impossible this time of year.
The tree's a maple! But looking
At the silhouette in evening,

I see a leopard in the tree:
A black figure limned on the blue
Horizon, hanging like a snake,
Coughing in the leafy branches,

A leopard weeping for its prey
As the twilight subsides, subsides.
Listen: those are kids on scooters
And a neighborly radio.

Look: a wife's walking down the street.
The air's as sweet as buttercups.
I won't be going out for tea.
A leopard's hanging in the tree.

Questions:
1. What do the various characters in the poem and their actions have to do with the leopard and its actions?
2. What is the tone of the poem and / or of the speaker?

Simone Muench

Pretty White Dress

Hey ladybird lurking,
what's a fuzzy to you

and a fizzy to him?
Calligraphy or filigree

on the shield of a Viking.
He's aloof as a sawtooth.

He can't yodel or sing.
He's a killer Godzilla,

a teapot signaling steam.
A telltale heart, a deadly dart.

It's a Harlequin romance,
a dizzy and a doozy of a dance.

He's a dense lens, a frigate
on a frozen ocean.

You're a whirl of a girl, pearl
and vertigo, marbled star.

He's a conversation in the dark

ardor or a parked car,

smelling of mint and gin
in a seaside citadel

gliding down your pretty
white dress with a pen.

Questions:
1. *What is the tone of this poem?*
2. *Is its content serious or unserious?*
3. *How do form and content work together here?*

Kimberly Johnson

Sonnet

No seduction in the hothouse, its aisles

of deliberate orchids only heave

beneath ceiling fans. The horticulturist's

a bawd-her monstrous offspring affront

with chromatic perfection, charm in array.

But when the orange orchard blossoms,

I am thrown.

Raptures in the garden? Never once did rows

of carrot so well-weeded yield

a swoon. Beware that flim-flam man,

the farmer, I grouse in passing, sowing

season by season an almanac theology.

But when orange blossoms wave

in pneumatic arcades, I dither. I coo. I hallelu.

Questions:
1. *Why is this poem called "Sonnet"?*
2. *What is the poem's tone?*
3. *Is the content serious or unserious?*

Eurydice & Loverboy

Hades is beautiful. We've our flowers, too,

in the weave of we've, in the blew of dark blue.

Lover boy! Look at you, spirit like dew,

even still, so self centered in your view.

Now your bones are dirt, the compost of my sky.

They live in a place where your flowers die

— it's a hard truth your flowers come to know,

each autumn when their petals let them go.

Not even men outlast themselves. Their wives

can, and do, go on, happy with their lives.

Is lover boy depressed? Does his heart feel black?

Well, just follow me, hon; I won't turn back.

Hades is beautiful. We've our flowers, too,

in the weave of we've, in the blew of dark blue.

Kim Addonizio

Echo and Narcissus

Poor love-struck Echo, stuck with repeating
everything he said. He might
have thought he deserved it,
to have a nymph for a girlfriend, who'd confirm

everything he said; he might
have loved how she mirrored him,
a girlfriend who'd say You're pretty
when he told her she was pretty,

who'd love him more than her mirror.
Not that they had mirrors in those days;
that was the problem. Anyway, she was pretty,
but he wasn't interested in nymphs.

If only they'd had mirrors in those days
he wouldn't have drowned in that reflecting pool,
finding it more interesting than nymphs.
But maybe he'd have beat his head against a mirror

and killed himself anyway, pool or no pool.
No free will in those days—it was all the gods.
You could beat your head against your fate, but still,
if you were Narcissus, you'd end up a white flower

stuck in the ground with no will, plucked or trampled by gods,

and someone would say it was deserved,

for beauty to come down to a white flower,

a poor echo, and someone's love stuck

in the ground, the ground, the ground, the ground.

Bruce Bond

Mercy

Dear happiness, forgive me;

you are not what I make histories of,

never the word inside my words:

the bright seed on the tongue

of the parakeet, lime green and chatty.

We both know you are nonsense mostly,

contrary to belief quite flightless

on your trapeze. Here now, you could be

the red worm burning in its peach;

even as I sink my teeth the blush

is fading into memoir. So it is with any star

eaten by the plain speech of day.

And what could be more fortunate,

which is why I know so little about you,

why I cannot repeat what I loved

more than these losses taken to heart.

We grow large in memory and sleep,

fluffing the pillows of our bodies,

our broken teeth turning to money:
I dreamt of you on a bicycle in the rain.
The sky was cloudless and shiny,

and I too was burning, a windy planet
liquid at the core, palmed in rain.
Then the dream was empty,

and there was only the body brimming over
with darkness, and I woke, speechless,
mouthing the sweet dark air of the room.

Question:
*Often, the point of a poem becomes most clear in its last lines. But where is
the point of "Mercy" most clear? How does the placement help us understand
the poem?*

Heather McHugh

Song for a Mountain Climber

Since fondness is rooted in folly,

shouldn't we should pray

that God's indifferent? Beyond

the fawning flock, past Everest and air,

shouldn't he stay a wholly yawning

dark? (The orders of indifference

more mightily amaze than those

of love. Love favors; love

excludes. On a lark, love tries

its millstone; on a sky its tint.

Love takes an object, takes a shine

to a calf whose gold its own eye-smitheries

have minted. Pure indifference

moves otherwise. It's unconditional:

a little fling cannot diminish it:

impartially it flies from everything-

from man's investments, and

his dearth.) The thought that God

might care for us is

terrifying: ought

to keep us hooked on earth.

Question:
*Where is the point of "Song for a Mountain Climber" most clear? How does
that placement help us understand the poem?*

Heather McHugh

Ill-Made Almighty

No man has more assurance than a bad poet.

-Martial

The logos thrives, it is crawling

with bugs. The lecturers, below,

are memorific, futurized, dead-certain

they'll go unsurprised. They don't

know nows as you do, true to no

clear destination. (You can't even act

your age, it's over-understudied.) Steady

as you go. The greatest waves are barely

bearable, alive's ill-read already,

and the Skipper is sick

of the terribly lit

graffiti in the head.

Margot Schilpp

Laws of My Nature

Obviously, the roosters are in league

with morning, the thrum of the sun

placing itself into the sky, again

the cholera, and again, mitosis—

electric salts of friction and desire

that appear out of nothing. Obviously

this happened, though as in dreams,

there are moments that feel

it might not have, not a dream, not a dream,

not anything, really, except disappearing

into silence. Regret is not a drug

I take and so I'm still sane. I am indigent,

which means to be in want, yet I want

for nothing. Another citadel of the skin,

another who can name me. Close by,

this waterfall carries breath.

I am enamored. A reverie continues.

Blue is an endearment, erratic

and sometimes missing. Let me decide
to speak, and then I am saying love,
I am saying again and everything and

absence, into the heavy air, almost
a fabrication of air, until it moves
into the lungs darkly. There is solace

in understatement, even if a thought
continues unsaid. There is the opposite
of clamor, and surely there is always

one feather spiraling on the wind.
I worry when things seem true,
and so disbelieve. I surrender

to the hardness of slate
and to the mossy places. Do you recognize
the markers of yearning in disguise?

Can you understand momentum
while you stand perfectly still?

A snake drops from the tree and makes

a small noise—the sound of thinking
itself away—and across the leaves
a slithering. My conscience must operate

that way—a long drop and then evasion—
because to understand how longing works
I would deny the sun its rising.

Assignment:

Examine and explain, in detail, how the principle of refrain—and of pattern in general—works in "Laws of My Nature."

Margot Schilpp

Manifesto

I know that dying is how we escape
the rest of our lives. I think that trees
send us a message: do not believe

you are lucky. The skins of apples
and the peeler will marry; it's simply
a question of when. Believe

in mourning and carrion birds.
Look how their fleshy treasures
dissolve in the sun before their very eyes.

To love something
you must have considered what it means
to do without. You must have thought

about it—the coefficient of the body
is another body—but do not forget
that there are people who are willing

to staple your palm to your chest.
Know there are places it isn't wise to go.
Begin again if you must: there are ways

to make up for what you have been before,
the dust in the corners that collects you.
Sympathy is overrated.

Rethink how lack
becomes everyone's master, drives us
into town and spends our money.

Quiet: the trees are napping.
Water meets itself again.
We reach for the days that precede us

and the world keeps us from knowing
too much. The body loves music,
the abandoned road of it;

each day a peel
lengthens in the shadow of blossoms,
fabric weaves itself into light.

Pay attention to the patterns. They repeat—
terraces erode, groves lie fallow—
order is cognate of joy.

Question:
How do image and abstraction complement each other in "Manifesto"?

R. T. Smith

Hardware Sparrows

Out for a deadbolt, light bulbs

and two-by-fours, I find a flock

of sparrows safe from hawks

and weather under the roof

of Lowe's amazing discount

store. They skitter from the racks

of stockpiled posts and hoses

to a spill of winter birdseed

on the concrete floor. How

they know to forage here,

I can't guess, but the automatic

door is close enough,

and we've had a week

of storms. They are, after all,

ubiquitous, though poor,

their only song an irritating

noise, and yet they soar

to offer, amid hardware, rope

and handyman brochures,
some relief, as if a flurry
of notes from Mozart swirled

from seed to ceiling, entreating
us to set aside our evening
chores and take grace where

we find it, saying it is possible,
even in this month of flood,
blackout and frustration,

to float once more on sheer
survival and the shadowy
bliss we exist to explore.

Questions:
*1. "Hardware Sparrows" describes a scene common to many, so where does
the poem get its uncommonness — its magic? Consider both form and content.
2. Are there any patterns in the poem?*

Mary Oliver

Poppies

The poppies send up their

orange flares; swaying

in the wind, their congregations

are a levitation

of bright dust, of thin

and lacy leaves.

There isn't a place

in this world that doesn't

sooner or later drown

in the indigos of darkness,

but now, for a while,

the roughage

shines like a miracle

as it floats above everything

with its yellow hair.

Of course nothing stops the cold,

black, curved blade

from hooking forward—

of course

loss is the great lesson.

But also I say this: that light

is an invitation

to happiness,

and that happiness,

when it's done right,

is a kind of holiness,

palpable and redemptive.

Inside the bright fields,

touched by their rough and spongy gold,

I am washed and washed

in the river

of earthly delight—

and what are you going to do—

what can you do

about it—

deep, blue night?

Linda Brewer

20 / 20

By the time they reached Indiana, Bill realized that Ruthie, his driving companion, was incapable of theoretical debate. She drove okay, she went halves on gas, etc., but she refused to argue. She didn't seem to know how. Bill was used to East Coast women who disputed everything he said, every step of the way. Ruthie stuck to simple observations, like "Look, cows." He chalked it up to the fact that she was from rural Ohio and thrilled to death to be anywhere else.

She didn't mind driving into the setting sun. The third evening out, Bill rested his eyes while she cruised along making the occasional announcement.

"Indian paintbrush. A golden eagle."

Miles later he frowned. There was no Indian paintbrush, that he knew of, near Chicago.

The next evening, driving, Ruthie said, "I never thought I'd see a Bigfoot in real life." Bill turned and looked at the side of the road streaming innocently out behind them. Two red spots winked back—reflectors nailed to a tree stump.

"Ruthie, I'll drive," he said. She stopped the car and they changed places in the light of the evening star.

"I'm so glad I got to come with you," Ruthie said. Her eyes were big, blue, and capable of seeing wonderful sights. A white buffalo near Fargo. A UFO above Twin Falls. A handsome genius in the person of Bill himself. This last vision came to her in Spokane and Bill decided to let it ride.

Assignment:
1. Interpret "20 / 20" using the psychological approach.
2. What other interpretive modes might be used to analyze the story? Write one interpretive summary for each applicable mode.

Daniel Orozco

Orientation

Those are the offices and these are the cubicles. That's
my cubicle there, and this is your cubicle. This is your phone.
Never answer your phone. Let the Voicemail System answer it.
This is your Voicemail System Manual. There are no personal
phone calls allowed. We do, however, allow for emergencies. If
you must make an emergency phone call, ask your supervisor
first. If you can't find your supervisor, ask Phillip Spiers who sits
over there. He'll check wil Clarissa Nicks, who sits over there.
If you make an emergency phone call without asking, you may
be let go.

These are your IN and OUT boxes. All the forms in your
IN box must be logged in by the date shown in the upper left-
hand corner, initialed by you in the upper right-hand corner, and
distributed to the Processing Analyst whose name is numerically
coded in the lower left-hand corner. The lower right-hand corner
is left blank. Here's your Processing Analyst Numerical Code
Index. And here's your Forms Processing Procedures Manual.

You must pace your work. What do I mean? I'm glad
you asked that. We pace our work according to the eight-hour
workday. If you have twelve hours of work in your IN box, for
example, you must compress that work into the eight-hour day.
If you have one hour of work in your IN box, you must expand
that work to fill the eight-hour day. That was a good question.
Feel free to ask questions. Ask too many questions, however, and
you may be let go.

That is our receptionist. She is a temp. We go through
receptionists here. They quit with alarming frequency. Be polite
and civil to the temps. Learn their names, and invite them to
lunch occasionally. But don't get close to them, as it only makes

it more difficult when they leave. And they always leave. You can be sure of that.

The men's room is over there. The women's room is over there. John LaFountaine, who sits over there, uses the women's room occasionally. He says it is accidental. We know better, but we let it pass. John LaFountaine is harmless, his forays into the forbidden territory of the women's room simply a benign thrill, a faint blip on the dull flat line of his life.

Russell Nash, who sits in the cubicle to your left, is in love with Amanda Pierce, who sits in the cubicle to your right. They ride the same bus together after work. For Amanda Pierce, it is just a tedious bus ride made less tedious by the idle nattering of Russell Nash. But for Russell Nash, it is the highlight of his day. It is the highlight of his life. Russell Nash has put on forty pounds, and grows fatter with each passing month, nibbling on chips and cookies while peeking glumly over the partitions at Amanda Pierce, and gorging himself at home on cold pizza and ice cream while watching adult videos on TV.

Amanda Pierce, in the cubicle to your right, has a six-year-old son named Jamie, who is autistic. Her cubicle is plastered from top to bottom with the boy's crayon artwork—sheet after sheet of precisely drawn concentric circles and ellipses, in black and yellow. She rotates them every other Friday. Be sure to comment on them. Amanda Pierce also has a husband, who is a lawyer. He subjects her to an escalating array of painful and humiliating sex games, to which Amanda Pierce reluctantly submits. She comes to work exhausted and freshly wounded each morning, wincing from the abrasions on her breasts, or the bruises on her abdomen, or the second-degree burns on the backs of her thighs.

But we're not supposed to know any of this. Do not let on. If you let on, you may be let go.

Amanda Pierce, who tolerates Russell Nash, is in love with Albert Bosch, whose office is over there. Albert Bosch, who only dimly registers Amanda Pierce's existence, has eyes only for Ellie Tapper, who sits over there. Ellie Tapper, who hates Albert Bosch, would walk through fire for Curtis Lance. But Curtis Lance hates Ellie Tapper. Isn't the world a funny place? Not in the ha-ha sense, of course.

Anika Bloom sits in that cubicle. Last year, while reviewing quarterly reports in a meeting with Barry Hacker, Anika Bloom's left palm began to bleed. She fell into a trance, stared into her hand, and told Barry Hacker when and how his wife would die. We laughed it off. She was, after all, a new employee. But Barry Hacker's wife is dead. So unless you want to know exactly when and how you'll die, never talk to Anika Bloom.

Colin Heavey sits in that cubicle over there. He was new once, just like you. We warned him about Anika Bloom. But at last year's Christmas Potluck, he felt sorry for her when he saw that no one was talking to her. Colin Heavey brought her a drink. He hasn't been himself since. Colin Heavey is doomed. There's nothing he can do about it, and we are powerless to help him. If he asks to do something tell him you have to check with me. If he asks again, tell him I haven't gotten back to you.

This is the Fire Exit. There are several on this floor, and they are marked accordingly. We have a Floor Evacuation Review every three months, and an Escape Route Quiz once a month. We have our Biannual Fire Drill twice a year, and our Annual Earthquake Drill once a year. These are precautions only. These things never happen.

For your information, we have a comprehensive health plan. Any catastrophic illness, any unforeseen tragedy is completely covered. All dependents are completely covered. Larry Bagdikian, who sits over there, has six daughters. If anything were to happen to any of his girls, or to all of them, if all six were to simultaneously fall victim to illness or injury — stricken with a hideous degenerative muscle disease or some rare toxic blood disorder, sprayed with semiautomatic gunfire while on a class field trip, or attacked in their bunk beds by some prowling nocturnal lunatic — if any of this were to pass, Larry's girls would all be taken care of. Lary Bagdikian would not have to pay one dime. He would have nothing to worry about.

We also have a generous vacation and sick leave policy. We have an excellent disability insurance plan. We have a stable and profitable pension fund. We get group discounts for the symphony, and block seating at the ballpark. We get commuter ticket books for the bridge. We have Direct Deposit. We are all members of Costco.

This is our kitchenette. And this, this is our Mr. Coffee. We have a coffee pool, into which we each pay two dollars a week for coffee, filters, sugar, and CoffeeMate. If you prefer Cremora or half-and-half to CoffeeMate, there is a special pool for three dollars a week. If you prefer Sweet'n Low to sugar, there is a special pool for two-fifty a week. We do not do decaf. You are allowed to join the coffee pool of your choice, but you are not allowed to touch the Mr. Coffee.

This is the microwave oven. You are allowed to *heat* food in the microwave oven. You are not allowed, however, to *cook* food in the microwave oven.

We get one hour for lunch. We also get one fifteen-minute break in the afternoon. Always take your breaks. If you skip a break, it is gone forever. For your information, your break is a privilege. If you abuse the lunch policy, our hands will be tied, and we will be forced to look the other way. We will not enjoy that.

This is the refrigerator. You may put your lunch in it.

Barry Hacker, who sits over there, steals food from this refrigerator. His petty theft is an outlet for his grief. Last New Year's Eve, while kissing his wife, a blood vessel burst in her brain. Barry Hacker's wife was two months pregnant at the time, and lingered in a coma for half a year before dying. It was a tragic loss for Barry Hacker. He hasn't been himself since. Barry Hacker's wife was a beautiful woman. She was also completely covered. Barry Hacker did not have to pay one dime. But his dead wife haunts him. She haunts all of us. We have seen her, reflected in the monitors of our computers, moving past our cubicles. We have seen the dim shadow of her face in our photocopies. She pencils herself in in the receptionist's appointment book, with the notation: To see Barry Hacker. She has left messages in the receptionst's Voicemail box, messages garbled by the electronic chirrups and buzzes in the phone line, her voice echoing from an immense distance within the ambient hum. But the voice is hers. And beneath her voice, beneath the tidal *whoosh* of static and hiss, the gurgling and crying of a baby can be heard.

In any case, if you bring a lunch, put a little something extra in the bag for Barry Hacker. We have four Barrys in this office. Isn't that a coincidence?

This is Matthew Payne's office. He is our Unit Manager, and his door is always closed. We have never seen him, and you will never see him. But he is here. You can be sure of that. He is all around us.

This is the Custodian's Closet. You have no business in the Custodian's Closet.

And this, this is our Supplies Cabinet. If you need supplies, see Curtis Lance. He will log you in on the Supplies Cabinet Authorization Log, then give you a Supplies Authorization Slip. Present your pink copy of the Supplies Authorization Slip to Ellie Tapper. She will log you in on the Supplies Cabinet

Key Log, then give you the key. Because the Supplies Cabinet is located outside the Unit Manager's office, you must be very quiet. Gather your supplies quietly. The Supplies Cabinet is divided into four sections. Section One contains letterhead stationery, blank paper and envelopes, memo and note pads, and so on. Section Two contains pens and pencils and typewriter and printer ribbons, and the like. In Section Three we have erasers, correction fluids, transparent tapes, glue sticks, et cetera. And in Section Four we have paper clips and push pins and scissors and razor blades. And here are the spare blades for the shredder. Do not touch the shredder, which is located over there. The shredder is of no concern to you.

Gwendolyn Stich sits in that office there. She is crazy about penguins, and collects penguin knickknacks: penguin posters and coffee mugs and stationery, penguin stuffed animals, penguin jewelry, penguin sweaters and T-shirts and socks. She has a pair of penguin fuzzy slippers she wears when working late at the office. She has a tape cassette of penguin sounds which she listens to for relaxation. Her favorite colors are black and white. She has personalized license plates that read PEN GWEN. Every morning, she passes through all the cubicles to wish each of us a *good* morning. She brings Danish on Wednesdays for Hump Day morning break, and doughnuts on Fridays for TGIF afternoon break. She organizes the Annual Christmas Potluck, and is in charge of the Birthday List. Gwendolyn Stich's door is always open to all of us. She will always lend an ear, and put in a good word for you; she will always give you a hand, or the shirt off her back, or a shoulder to cry on. Because her door is always open, she hides and cries in a stall in the women's room. And John LaFountaine — who, enthralled when a woman enters, sits quietly in his stall with his knees to his chest — John LaFountaine has heard her vomiting in there. We have come upon Gwendolyn

Stich huddled in the stairwell, shivering in the updraft, sipping a Diet Mr. Pibb and hugging her knees. She does not let any of this interfere with her work. If it interfered with her work, she might have to be let go.

Kevin Howard sits in that cubicle over there. He is a serial killer, the one they call the Carpet Cutter, responsible for the mutilations across town. We're not supposed to know that, so do not let on. Don't worry. His compulsion inflicts itself on strangers only, and the routine established is elaborate and unwavering. The victim must be a white male, a young adult no older than thirty, heavyset, with dark hair and eyes, and the like. The victim must be chosen at random, before sunset, from a public place; the victim is followed home, and must put up a struggle, et cetera. The carnage inflicted is precise: the angle and direction of the incisions; the layering of skin and muscle tissue; the rearrangement of the visceral organs; and so on. Kevin Howard does not let any of this interfere with his work. He is, in fact, our fastest typist. He types as if he were on fire. He has a secret crush on Gwendolyn Stich, and leaves a red-foil-wrapped Hershey's Kiss on her desk every afternoon. But he hates Anika Bloom, and keeps well away from her. In his presence, she has uncontrollable fits of shaking and trembling. Her left palm does not stop bleeding.

In any case, when Kevin Howard gets caught, act surprised. Say that he seemed like a nice person, a bit of a loner, perhaps, but always quiet and polite.

This is the photocopier room. And this, this is our view. It faces southwest. West is down there, toward the water. North is back there. Because we are on the seventeenth floor, we are afforded a magnificent view. Isn't it beautiful? It overlooks the park, where the tops of those trees are. You can see a segment of the bay between those two buildings there. You can see the sun set in the gap between those two buildings over there. You can see this building reflected in the glass panels of that building across the way. There. See? That's you, waving. And look there. There's Anika Bloom in the kitchenette, waving back.

Enjoy this view while photocopying. If you have problems with the photocopier, see Russell Nash. If you have any questions, ask your supervisor. If you can't find your supervisor, ask Phillip Spiers. He sits over there. He'll check with Clarissa Nicks. She sits over there. If you can't find them, feel free to ask me. That's my cubicle. I sit in there.

Questions:
1. *How does the story's form further its content?*
2. *In poetry we often find the volta—a turn or shift; how does "Orientation" use turns or shifts?*
3. *What interpretive modes would be most helpful to understanding the story, and why?*

Jonathan Goldstein

Man Not Superman

She missed normal men. Lois wanted someone normal. That's how I won over a class act like Lois Lane — it was the fact that I was a mere mortal.

She had had her fill of the night rides over Metropolis on Superman's back. She had done the demystifying "I'm-letting-you-get-toknow-the-real-me" trips to the Fortress of Solitude. He had even taken her to Niagara Falls to see the statues made of wax that honored him there, and because she insisted, they took the train. That drove him crazy. At one point, as the conductor punched his ticket, he turned to Lois and said, "Do you have any idea how ridiculous this is for me?" And then he laughed. He laughed because he loved her. Despite all of this, she had still decided to leave him.

I first met Lois at a charity penny arcade event. At one point in the evening, as I stood hunched over a pinball machine, I looked over to my side, and there was Lois Lane just standing there, watching me. The left flipper wasn't working, so I tried to keep the ball on the right, but when it came down the left, we yelled like a couple of kids rolling down the side of a mountain together.

"I've always wanted to reach in there and hold the silver ball in my hand," I said.

"I never thought of it that way," said Lois, and five minutes later she was ripping open an empty pack of Clorets and writing her number down on the white inside.

Lois was the kind of woman I had always dreamed of. Even her name — so cool and crisp — Lois Lane. It pierced my ear like an arrow. Lois was the kind of woman who made you feel like "I am a man who dates Lois Lane," and as simple as that sounds, it is the best way I can describe it.

When I was a child, she was the girl who brought Oreos for lunch, the one who during recess held me cruelly aloft on the seesaw as I squirmed and begged to be let down. In high school, she was the popular girl who wanted nothing to do with me, who saw me as nothing more than a bad aftertaste — like the kind you get when you almost vomit, and can taste the vomit, but don't actually vomit. In college, Lois was the bored coquette, languidly offering me her leg in the cafeteria, saying, "Feel how strong my calf muscles are." Lois was all of these, but then, at the moment she handed me her phone number, she became something else entirely. She became a woman who had chosen me.

At first I was a novelty. In the beginning, Lois would kiss my forehead and tell me she loved how *squishy* my arms were. "In a good way," she'd say. "They're so easy to fall asleep on."

In front of Lois, I wasn't embarrassed by my softness. In fact, all the things my old girlfriends had found unattractive and gross about me, she found charming.

Once, I even gave my nipples eyelashes and smeared lipstick around my belly button. Lois swooned as I made my fat gut sing her sweet songs of love.

I liked making Lois laugh. One evening I even purchased a jar of olives simply because one of them, pressed up against the glass, looked like an old man's head, with a little skewed stroke-mouth full of pimento. I gave it a voice. I made it say things like "Get me out of here," and "My ass is asleep," and Lois appeared to find this delightful.

Although they were broken up, Lois and Superman decided to remain friends, and since they traveled in the same circles, I knew it would be only a matter of time before Superman and I met, and I knew that when we did, by any possible system of measurement, he would destroy me.

But in what way, I wondered. I mean, what could he do to me? Squeeze my hand really hard when we said hello? No: he could out-fight me, out-think me, out-run me, out-fly me — he could reverse time, for Christ's sake!

Lois told me that I should expect a call from Superman. She said he was really anxious to meet me, and several weeks into our relationship, I got the call. When I answered the phone, I felt my chest tighten.

"I'd like to keep Lois in my life," he said, "and I guess that means we should get to know each other. I don't want to make this into a big deal or anything, but Lois tells me you're sort of between jobs right now, and I could use a sidekick. I'm trying to change my image a little. I don't want to come off as such a lone wolf anymore. It would be part-time, and I could teach you a thing or two."

"Look, don't get me wrong," I said. "You do great things. Wonderful things ...."

"Silence," he said, but he didn't say it in the way you'd think, all capital letters; he said it quietly, sadly almost. "Silence. Just think about it."

When I saw Lois that night for dinner, she had already spoken to Superman, and she was going on about my sidekick-ship like it was already a done deal.

"It's just what you need to get back into the workforce," she said, and she looked so pleased. Before I knew it, we were drinking glass after glass of red wine, and I was agreeing that it might be a good idea. Lois is just so beautiful when she's pleased.

The next morning, I met Superman for lunch, and before I could sit down in the booth, he handed me a rumpled paper bag.

"What's this?" I asked.

"Your new outfit," he said.

He shooed me off to the bathroom, and in the toilet stall I changed into what was essentially a skintight black unitard. There was no cape. The whole thing succeeded in making me look both skinny-legged and rotund around the middle. Across the chest, in small Courier font, was the word *Stuart*.

I pointed at the name questioningly as I walked back to the table.

"It's your sidekick name," Superman said. "And you're not supposed to wear your uniform with underwear."

I spent most of my time wearing my Stuart outfit in Superman's apartment, ironing his costume, fielding calls from the press, and popping boils on his back with a nail and an atlas. In between, Superman had me doing nonstop situps. He called my gut "a crime against humanity." His favorite joke was to put his hand on my stomach and ask, "How many months?"

But he wasn't perfect, either. Up close Superman stank of Brylcreem, and when he was being all solemn, he would use words like *shall* and *vex*. He was also really full of himself. At one point he even told me I should use the word *super* sparingly. He said its use was only appropriate when describing works of God or Superman's own feats and properties.

Through all of his talk, I would try to maintain eye contact with him, and as I did, I would think to myself, "I have seen Lois in her underwear, and tonight, when I go home, I might see her in her underwear some more."

I wouldn't put it past the bastard to read minds.

As horrible as it all got, in the evening there was Lois, and she seemed so proud of me. Still, Superman was a constant, unspoken presence between us. I always knew he was out there, feeling *better* than me. And when I looked at Lois sometimes, I knew she knew I was thinking it, and I guess it made her want to think about it a little herself.

It all came to a head one Thursday night. There was this Thursday-night tradition where all the superheroes got together for beer and chicken wings, and on this particular evening, Lois was going to join us. The superheroes sat together at one table, capes all undone, laughing and slapping each other on the back, while the sidekicks sat at another table, commiserating and trash talking.

I looked around my table. There was the angry-looking hunchback the Green Lantern worked with, and Wonder Woman had brought along a sad-eyed, mousy college-aged girl who sketched on napkins all night. The Flash had taken on this grizzled old sack of bones whom he called Benjamin and who smelled of cabbage and urine. Superman told me Benjamin was the Flash's father, and he needed some looking after. The Flash mainly left him in the car.

And then, of course, there was Batman's sidekick, Robin. Robin told me that the Caped Crusader was such a control freak he had continued to bathe Robin well into his late teens.

"I can scrub my own ass," Robin would yell, but Batman was so strong. When he put his hand on Robin's shoulder, Robin wasn't going *anyplace*.

I looked over at Superman chatting with Batman, the best of buddies, and I imagined what their conversation was like on the night they had heard about me and Lois.

It was as I sat there, imagining the two of them laughing at me, their massive upper torsos jerking in an impossibly manly manner, that I saw Lois walk in. Superman caught her eye, and she made a beeline for him. Instinctively, I rose from my seat.

Superman turned to me, and our eyes locked.

Much has been written about Superman, but there is an aspect of him that is very difficult to describe. There is a certain feeling one gets when looking into his eyes, and of all the articles I have read, there isn't one that touches on it. It's inhuman and hypnotic, but it's not just that. Being looked at by Superman makes you feel more *there* than even a dozen TV cameras. And it's not simply that you're *there*, but that you're there swaddled in fur coats while sipping warm cider. It's comfy and cozy, and I cannot explain it well enough.

When she kissed Superman's cheek hello, I got up and walked out of the bar. Because I was in my Stuart outfit, I didn't even have pockets to dig my fists into.

Some time after one in the morning, Lois showed up at my place full of apologies. She said she had gone over to sit with me, but that I had already left. She had spent the whole night talking with Superman. She said that he was really depressed.

"I've never seen him like this. I'm actually a bit worried," she said. "He's obsessed with the emptiness of the universe. He said that after we broke up, he went looking for God — literally *looking* for God, zipping across the universe — and he came up with nothing."

I wasn't in the mood for a big Superman-is-a-man-of-constant-sorrow routine, but she was clearly on a roll, and I didn't have the heart to stop her.

"I never realized how obsessive he can be. He told me there was once a certain way I flipped my hair that so beguiled him he spun around the earth reversing the moment 75,000 times. I never knew that."

I felt myself grow queasy.

"He's just so intense," she continued, "and this planet can be so cold. Did you know that on Krypton, when two people fell in love, they became inseparable? They even had special clothes they wore together, and they learned to move together in unison. He said that on Earth these kinds of garments have names like Fundies and are sold only in the pages of pornographic magazines. He said Earth is a sick, sick place."

My fear wasn't that Lois would get back together with Superman — because by this point I knew it was only a matter of time before she would — but that she would describe the summer we spent together as the most miserable, depressing, and disgusting time of her life. I already knew how it would infuriate him. I could hear him making his stupid jock jokes with her: "You don't need super-vision to see through that sap," he would say.

After she left my apartment, I decided to take a walk to clear my head. I did so while cursing Superman until there were tears in my eyes. I had walked only a couple of blocks when I ran into Clark Kent.

I had been introduced to Clark at a couple of Lois's soirees and, although I hardly knew him, he was someone I really liked. He possessed what I felt — from my *citified* point of view — was genuine small-town warmth, and I just enjoyed being around it.

He told me I looked terribly sad. *Terribly sad.* People didn't say stuff like that anymore. Having him call me *terribly sad* instead of *depressed* or *bummed* made me start to feel a little bit better. He asked me if I wanted to grab a beer, and I said sure.

I told Clark all about the evening, and he listened to me. That was all I really needed just then: to be listened to.

"How do you know she'll go running back to Superman?" asked Clark.

"You should hear her talk," I said. "Do you have any

idea how much Superman can bench press? Superman once went back in time and beat up Hitler. I mean, who can compete with that?"

Clark started laughing so hard that people at the other tables turned around to look at us. I was on a roll. With his laughter egging me on, I told him all the things that over the last few weeks I wished I had said to Superman.

"You're such a phony," I said. "You have this idea of what it means to be human, but it's a parody. Humans feel pain, and you don't understand what pain is. You may be super, but you are certainly not a man."

Clark thought that was just perfect. He put his arm around my neck and rocked me back and forth as we both laughed.

Question:
As you know, one of the functions of fiction is to entertain. "Man Not Superman" certainly entertains. But doesn't it also teach? What are the lessons in it?

John McPhee

In Virgin Forest

In virgin forest, the ground is uneven, dimpled with pits
and adjacent mounds. Perfect trees rise, yes, with boles clear
to fifty and sixty feet; but imperfect trees are there too—bent
twigs, centuries after bending—not to mention the dead stand-
ing timber, not to mention four thousand board feet rotting as
one trunk among the mayapples and the violets: a toppled hull
fruited with orange-and-cream fungi, which devour the wood,
metabolize it, cause it literally to disappear. In virgin forest, the
classic symbol of virginity is a fallen uprooted trunk decaying
in a bed of herbs.

In our latitude, the primeval forest would include
grapes, their free-floating vines descending like bridge cables.
Wild grapes are incapable of climbing trees. They are lifted by
trees as the trees grow, and their bunches hang from the top of
the canopy. In our latitude, there is a great scarcity of virgin
forest. Cut the grapevines, make a few stumps, let your cattle in
to graze, and it's all over till the end of time. Nonetheless, we
were in such a place a few days ago, and did not have to travel
far to see it. Never cut, never turned, it was a piece of American
deciduous forest in continuous evolution dating to the tundras
of mesolithic times. Some of the trees were ninety feet tall, with
redtails nesting in them, and when the hawks took off and rose
above the canopy they could see the World Trade Center.

We had made our way to Franklin Township, New
Jersey, which includes New Brunswick and is one of the less
virgin milieus in America. This is where the megalopolis came
in so fast it trapped animals between motels. It missed, though,
half a mile of primeval woods. The property, a little east of
East Millstone, was settled in 1701 by Mynheer Cornelius Van

Liew and remained in one family for two hundred and fifty-four years. They cleared and farmed most of their land but consciously decided to leave sixty-five acres untouched. The Revolution came and went, the Civil and the World Wars, but not until the nineteen-fifties did the family seek the counsel of a sawyer. The big trees were ruled by white oaks, dating to the eighteenth and seventeenth centuries, and their value was expressible in carats. Being no less frank than Dutch, the family lets its intentions be known. As often will happen in conservation crises, this brought forth a paradox of interested parties: rod-and-gun groups, the Nature Conservancy, the Adirondack Mountain Club, the United Daughters of the Confederacy. A tract of virgin forest is so rare that money was raised in thirty-eight states and seven foreign countries. But not enough. The trees were worth a good deal more. In the end, the forest was saved by, of all people, the United Brotherhood of Carpenters and Joiners of America, whose president remarked in 1955, as he handed over the property to Rutgers University, "What happens in the woodlands is close to the carpenter's heart."

Named for a Brotherhood president, the tract is called Hutcheson Memorial Forest. A brief trail makes a loop near one end. The deed limits Rutgers to that, and Rutgers is not arguing. The university's role is to protect the periphery and to study the woods. When something attacks, Rutgers makes notes. A disease that kills American beeches is on its way from Maine. "The forest deed says basically you don't do anything about it," a biologist named Edmund Stiles explained to us. "You watch what happens." In 1981, gypsy moths tore off the canopy, and sunlight sprayed the floor. The understory thickened as shrubs and saplings responded with a flush of growth. "The canopy is now closing over again," Stiles went on. "There's a real patchwork nature in an old forest, in the way it is always undergoing replacement." He stopped to admire a small white ash standing alone beneath open sky. "That's going to take the canopy," he said. "It's going all the way. It has been released. It will fill the gap."

Forty-two years old and of middle height—wearing boots, bluejeans, a brown wool shirt—Stiles had a handsome set of muttonchops and a tumble of thick brown hair that flowed over his forehead toward inquiring blue eyes. He had been working in Hutcheson Forest for thirteen years, he told us, and had recently become director. His doctoral disseration, at the University of Washington, was on bird communities in alder forests. More recently, he had studied the foraging strategies of insects and the symbiotic relationships of berries and migratory birds. In other words, he was a zoologist and a botanist, too. From secretive gray foxes to the last dead stick—that was what the untouched forest was about. The big oaks (red, white, and black), the shagbark hickories, sugar maples, beeches, ashes, and dogwoods—among thousands of plant and animal species—were only the trees.

As we talked, and moved about, tasting the odd spicebush leaf or a tendril of smilax, Stiles divided his attention and seemed not to miss a sound. "Spicebush and dogwood fruits are very high in lipids," he said. "They are taken on by birds getting ready for long migratory flights. Those are wood thrushes calling. A forest has to be at least a hundred years old to get a wood thrush. Actually, it takes about four centuries to grow a forest of this kind. The gap phenomenon is typical of old forest. There's a white-eyed vireo. Blue-winged warbler. There are cycles of openness and closedness in the canopies. Trees take advantage. Fill in the gaps. These are white-oak seedlings from a mast year. There's a nice red-bellied woodpecker." He was like Toscanini, just offstage, listening idly to his orchestra as it tuned itself up.

He said he had developed a theory that out-of-season splotches of leaf color are messages to frugivorous birds—the scattered early orange among sassafras leaves of the wild strawberry, the red of the Virginia creeper when everything else is green. When fruit is ready, the special colors turn on. He heard a great crested flycatcher. He bent down to a jack-in-the-pulpit, saying that it bears bird-disseminated fruit and is pollinated by a small black fly.

German foresters who came to visit Hutcheson Forest have been surprised by the untidiness of the place, startled by the jumble of life and death. "These Germans are unfamiliar with stuff just lying around, with the truly virginal aspect of the forest," Stiles said. Apparently, the Germans, like almost everyone else, had a misconception of forest primeval—a picture of Wotan striding through the noonday twilight, of Ludwig D. Boone shouting for *Lebensraum* among giant columns of uniform trees. "You don't find redwoods," Stiles said summarily. "You don't find Evangeline's forest. You find a more realistic forest."

You find a huge white ash that has grown up at an angle of forty-five degrees, and in a managed forest would have long ago been tagged for destruction. You find remarkably deep humus. You find a great rusty stump, maybe six feet high, and jagged where the trunk now beside it snapped off. More often, you find whole root structures tipped into the air and looking like radial engines. As you will nowhere else, you find the topography of pits and mounds. In its random lumpiness, it could be a model of glacial terrain. When a tree goes over and its roots come ripping from the ground, they bring with them a considerable mass of soil. When the tree has disappeared, the dirt remains as a mound, which turns kelly green with moss. Beside it is the pit that the roots came from. When no other trace remains of the tree, you can see by the pit and the

mound the direction in which the tree fell, and guess
its approximate size. If cattle graze in pit-and-mound
topography, they trample and destroy it. The pits and
mounds of centuries are evidence of virgin forest.

There is supporting evidence in human records
and in tree rings. People from Columbia's Lamong-
Doherty Geological Observatory have cored some trees
in Hutcheson Forest and dated them, for example to
1699, 1678. Neighboring land was settled, and cleared
for farming, in 1701. Lamont-Doherty has an ongoing
project called the Easter Network Dendrochronology
Series, which has sought and catalogued virgin stands at
least two hundred and fifty years old. The list is short
and scattered, and the tracts are small, with the notable
exceptions of Joyce Kilmer Memorial Forest, in North
Carolina (thirty-eight hundred virgin acres), the cove
hardwoods of Great Smoky Mountains National Park,
and a large stand of hemlocks and beeches in Allegheny
National Forest, in western Pennsylvania. There are
three hundred virgin acres on the Wabash River in Illi-
nois, and, in eastern Ohio, a woods of white oaks some
of which were seedlings when the Pilgrims reached New
England. The Ohio white oaks, like the white oaks of
Hutcheson Forest, are from three to four feet in diameter.
Old white oaks are found in few places, because they
had a tendency to become bowsprits, barrel staves, and
queenpost trusses. Virgin hemlocks are comparatively
common. Maine is not rich in virgin timber—some red
spruce on Mt. Katahdin, some red spruce above Tunk
Lake. There is a river gorge in Connecticut where trees
have never been cut. Some red spruce and hemlock in
the Adirondacks date to the late fifteen-hundreds, and

the hemlocks of the Allegheny forest are nearly two centuries
older than that. In the Shawangunk Mountains, about seventy
miles northwest of our office on Forty-third Street, is the oldest
known stand of pitch pine (360 years), also some white pine
(370), chestnut oak (330), and eastern hemlock (500). They are
up on a quartzite ridge line, though, and are very slow-growing
small trees. Remnant old-growth stands tend to be in moun-
tains, in rocky craggy places, not in flatlands. Hutcheson Forest,
in the Newark Basin, — in what was once a prime piedmont
area — is thus exceptionally rare. In the region of New York City,
there is nothing like it, no other clearly documented patch. In
fact, it is the largest mixed-oak virgin forest left in the eastern
United States.

Running through the forest is Spooky Brook, spawning
ground of the white sucker. Rutgers would like to control the
headwaters, fearing something known as herbicide drift. Con-
tinuing population drift is no less a threat, as development fills
in lingering farms. The woods are closed to visitors, except
for scheduled Sunday tours. Rutgers already owns some hun-
dred and fifty acres contiguous to the forest, and hopes, with
the help of the Nature Conservancy, to get two hundred more.
Manipulative research is carried out on the peripheral land,
while observational research goes on in the forest, which has
been described by Richard Forman, a professor at Harvard, as
"propbably the single most studied primeval woods on the con-
tinent." People have gone in there and emerged with more
than a hundred advanced degrees, including thirty-six Ph.D.s.
So many articles, papers, theses, and other research publications
have come out of Hutcheson Forest that countless trees have
been clear-cut elsewhere just in order to print them.

1987

Exercises:

1. *Highlight in one color the most poetic, image- and rhythm-driven passages of "In Virgin Forest," and highlight in a second color the more straightforward, data-driven passages.*

2. *Summarize the pattern that emerges; write a paragraph or two explaining how McPhee balances the lyrical with the prosaic.*

3. *In paragraph six we see an intermingling of narration with depiction, an effective melding of form and content. Underline the passages that are McPhee's narration—his telling—of his interview with Stiles, and box in the passages where McPhee shows us Stiles acting out McPhee's narration. Summarize how McPhee animates what he reports.*

4. *Identify and discuss similes, refrains, and other literary devices in the essay.*

Assignment:

Write your own essay in the style of "In Virgin Forest." Use the McPhee essay as your model for structure and balance. You are aiming for a descriptive essay that also informs. What follows on the next pages is an example of this—one student's essay response to this assignment.

Reyna Cardenas

The Giving Field

In the giving field, the furrows are alive, full of plants and humble workers. There are empty furrows, yes, waiting to be planted in; but there is lush vegetation too. From it spring juicy strawberries lightly hanging from the little plants, the fresh leafy lettuce, and the globes of artichokes, and in the furrows hopeful people are ready to harvest it all. In the giving field, the classic symbol of giving is a bare plant after a field worker has taken its offspring.

If the good people of the planet had the option today, even Death Valley would be a giving field, full of potatoes, lettuce, carrots, cauliflower, and others, even fruits like strawberries. But this is a fantasy. The real fields are defenseless, at the mercy of people, defenseless like children against monsters. If we destroy the land that gives birth to the different vegetables and fruits to make more space for stores, houses, and buildings, our valley may become nothing but concrete. Then where would we grow our food? Yet the fields are not completely alone. Even though there are short-sighted people who wish to get rid of all the giving fields, there are also humble people willing to take care of the fields like a father takes care of his children. However, they cannot defend the fields alone. Like a father needs the help of his wife to protect his children, the field workers need the help of other community members to protect the fields. Let's not let strangers take over the land, child of us who live here. Let's not lose the heart of our valley, our beautiful giving fields.

For the people of Salinas Valley, every day on the way to work it is easy to see the tons of varied greens in the giving field, and to smell the fresh strawberries along the road sides, without realizing that other people do not have this privilege, that there are people who have never seen the beauty of the fields. How could anyone live without the views of the sunrise shining on the giving fields each morning? On the east coast of our country, for example, many teenagers do not even know from where their vegetables come.

A year ago a group of high school students from New York came to my high school, Salinas High, to learn how the vegetables grow in our fields. They approached my friend Guadalupe and me because our parents work in the fields, and since we were part of the immigrant program from school, they thought we might know something about the subject. I had thought that I did not know much about agriculture, but I was wrong—these high school students thought that lettuce grows on trees! The visiting students knew numbers and statistics about Salinas' prosperity, but when they actually saw how the people work to get the produce from the land, they were captivated. Through no fault of their own, the only thing they had known before was that our valley is famous for its variety of vegetables, but the students' young faces, and their readiness to learn everything about these fields that provide the world with its delicious culinary necessities, motivated me to appreciate our giving fields even more.

Salinas Valley is known as the Salad Bowl of the World, and perhaps there is more than one good reason for this name. Walking through the furrows, feeling the dirt under your bare feet, touching the plants with your hands, feeling the wind pulling back your hair, and smelling the sweetness of the lettuce makes you believe the world has no end. This feeling reminds us that our Salad Bowl of the World not only provides sustenance; it also revitalizes us. When the students from the east coast, my friend, and I were in the fields, I saw how they were revitalized too; their faces lighted up and their eyes widened when they saw the never ending field. They spread out to smell the strawberries like bees collecting nectar. I asked them what they thought about the field, and they said that they could not believe how they could have gone through life without actually seeing it. Now there are people in other states who appreciate the giving fields—maybe even more than some people who live here in the valley do.

Not all people appreciate the importance of the giving fields. The monster of industry wants to destroy the fields and make more buildings in order to make more money. The city of Salinas is quickly growing, and that means more stores and other buildings are being constructed. Ettinger reports that while the population of Salinas in 2000 was 134,680, by 2020, the population of Monterey County will increase 37% to 537,000 people, with urban population increasing by 23,800 people (Ettinger, 2002). There is nothing wrong with people wanting to move here, to Salinas, but a variety of industries see relocation here simply as an opportunity to make a profit. Right now Monterey County is the third largest agriculture-producing county in the state (Ettinger, 2002). By destroying the fields to make room for new construction, industry is also shifting the economy. The demand for produce is increasing, but there is not enough land on which to grow the produce because buildings are being constructed; consequently, the price of produce is increasing even more.

People come to Salinas to tend the giving land and build better lives. Ironically, if the land is replaced by stores and malls, there will be less and less work for people. Every day, with the hope of obtaining something in return, many rough hands harvest the Salinas Valley fields for our meals. These humble people hope for the opportunity to give their families a better life. They may not have attended school, but they know that they cannot take for granted the simple things in life. Those hands understand that we cannot live without the giving fields.

As the high school students were finishing their tour here in Salinas and getting back in the school bus for home, they told me that they would never forget the sun setting down on the ocean of green vegetation. This experience not only taught them the wonderful things that the fields do for the world; it also taught me that we cannot forget about these fields, and that we all should feel proud of living among the giving fields. Many people, such as members of the Nature Institute and Action for Nature, want to protect these giving fields against the monster of industry, and we should help them in any way we can. We must strike a balance between new things and the things we need to preserve. We need our giving fields because we need and enjoy different fruits and vegetables, yes, but thanks to our giving fields we can also enjoy the clean air and the healthy life that those who live surrounded only by buildings we will never experience.

Salinas is not the only giving field. There are many others, and all of them give and give without asking anything in return. That does not mean we should not honor them.

Work Cited

Ettinger, Amy. "Salinas, CA. Face Squeeze From Housing Crunch." Monterey County Herald. June 19, 2002. Retrived from: http://ea.pomona.edu/salinasag.html

Basic Composition: The Body Paragraph Format

The student essay "Wake up People, Please!" appears on the following pages. Read the essay in its entirety for content, then reread it for form, this time with pen in hand, performing these tasks:

1. Box in the thesis statement.

2. Underline each topic sentence.

3. Put parentheses around body paragraph summary sentences.

4. With a highlighter or colored ink pen, circle the entire hook.

5. With that same highlighter or colored ink pen, place a squiggly line beneath the punchline.

6. WIth a RED ink pen, mark any areas you don't understand — grammar, vocabulary, sentence structure, et cetera, and bring a list of questions about these things to class.

Next, answer these questions:

What is the essay's main purpose: to express oneself, to inform others, or to persuade others?

Does the essay achieve its purpose? If it were your essay, would you add or change anything? If not, why not? If so, explain what you would do and why.

Negar Adeli

Wake up People, Please!

The world has changed dramatically over the last century. Computers, for example, play such a big role in our lives that we often hear our most important news on the Internet. One beautiful April morning, I got on the Internet to check my email and the news around the globe. In my mailbox was an email from one of my friends in Iran. Casually, I thought "Oh, let's see what they are doing over there." As I began to read the email, I started to get a bit nervous and confused. I was soon shocked to learn that my best friend had passed away. As the email said, some events in life are too painful to believe, but sadly are real. What bothers me the most is that my friend was not sick, nor was she in a car accident or anything like that; rather, she had committed suicide at the age of nineteen. I was unable to comprehend how a person like her had convinced herself to leave this world, but I was sure it must have been something hard to bear that drove her to commit such an act. Although the world has changed dramatically over the last hundred or so years, some things have remained the same. Kate Chopin's *The Awakening*, written in the 1890s, is a story pointing out a serious problem with which my friend was also faced: throughout history, women have held less power than men. This results in women having limited options for coping with their difficulties, which may lead them to perceive their choices as few and extreme—such as suicide, in some cases. By depicting the problems women faced a century ago, the story of Edna Pontellier in Chopin's novel reminds us of issues that are still unresolved in our society today, and shows us how tragic the consequences of ignoring these issues might be.

The Awakening is the tale of a young, free-spirited woman who is married to an older rich man. What a surprise!

Yet this woman is not like other women of her time. She does not care much about cooking and cleaning or satisfying the ever-changing needs of her man. She wants to be herself and pursue whatever makes her heart beat faster—which is great, but is she able to do that? No, she can not achieve what she wants because everyone around her insists that she is not capable of doing so. No one in her life supports her in defining herself and deciding her own destiny.

Edna Pontellier has two kids and a husband, but she never feels as if they are everything she could ever want. Edna's marriage is not ideal for her. She married Leonce for two reasons: first, to rebel against her family's wishes; second, because "his absolute devotion flattered her" (Chopin 32). There is no mutual love strengthening the marriage, which leaves Edna longing for something more. Her husband does not remain the devoted lover either. He is usually away from home on trips for work, and when he is in town, he goes out to enjoy activities without Edna. He makes the decisions for the household, and although that is the expected norm at that time, Edna does not agree with the power he possesses over her life. Leonce thinks of Edna as an object, and he takes care of his wife mainly so that she can keep his kids happy and most importantly look happy in front of everyone. The only thing he cares about is how people perceive their life. When Edna starts to wake up from her lifelong dream and discover herself as an individual, he worries that she is crazy. Too free-spirited to accept the typical roles for women in her society, she is not a "mother woman"—a woman who feels completely happy and satisfied merely to care for her children and husband and have no other real interests—yet she claims that she would give her life for her children. She would give her life, she explains, but she would never sacrifice *herself*. This shows what a strong individual she is. She knows she is an individual behind all the responsibilities and labels she has as a mother and a wife. She has her own interests and her own self-developing personality.

One cause of Edna's awakening is her relationship with a young man named Robert. The story revolves around their relationship. Robert is around Edna's age and shares similar interests with her. Although he makes her heart beat faster, he causes some problems too. In Edna's era, divorce is taboo, so if Edna leaves her husband to be with Robert, it means leaving the whole society. On the other hand, if she leaves Robert, that means leaving her passion and happiness. Ultimately, however, Edna does not get to make that decision either—Robert makes the decision, against her wishes, showing himself to be just another man who thinks Edna is incapable of making choices for herself. Although she realizes that she is above needing a man in order to be happy and that she would forget about Robert after a while, Edna is deeply hurt to discover that Robert, the one man she believed respected her, makes what should have been a mutual decision without her. This event makes her realize how helpless she is in determining her own destiny.

The society is portrayed through Edna's friends as well as through her family and Robert. Edna's friends are mother women—they care mainly about their families. They do not know who they really are; rather, they think of themselves only as caretakers. They consider themselves perfectly normal and see Edna as the alien one. Edna is not like them, and that creates a problem for her. Even though Edna is right to seek her individuality, everyone else opposes her and that makes her seem like the one at fault.

Edna's husband, 'boyfriend,' friends, and community in general are essentially the antagonists to what Edna thinks of herself and what she wants to be. She wants to find happiness by being herself and going after what/whom she loves, but she can't because no one has her back; she is one strong individual, but her entire society thinking of her as wrong and incapable of managing herself is a constant force working against her. Her society offers her very few options, and whichever she chooses, she will lose herself. If she chooses her husband, she can not go after what/whom she loves, and her destiny will be controlled by Leonce. If she chases after Robert and insists on reversing his decision, she ultimately will not want to stay with him since he had shown such disrespect for her. She could find some other guy but would always have the feeling that if Robert could betray her, anybody could. If she simply leaves her husband, she leaves behind her children and thereby leaves her family shamed to have had a wife/mother choose a life alone over one with them. She cannot save herself since she does not have the power to make choices for herself, and if she tries to make her own choices, everyone in the society will make her life a living hell by criticizing her for not being an obedient wife, a good mother-woman, and so on. Everyone in the story, just like most every person in Edna's era, is antagonistic to Edna's attempts to live her own life, to be an individual.

There is one other choice for Edna, and she takes it. By killing herself she finds what appears to be the only way she can assert her independence without interference from others. We may think Edna's choice wrong, yet do we ask ourselves what Edna's 'society' might have done wrong, or differently? My friend killed herself only three months ago. The reason she chose not to live anymore was to escape the situation where she did not have any say in what she did. She did not have the power to decide for herself, and sadly, she saw her only alternative as suicide. Everyday I wish I had been in Iran at that time to convince her otherwise, but it is too late now. *Could* I have convinced her anyway? Or does there need to be more change, by many more people willing to work to resolve unfair situations such as the one my friend was in?

We all need to work to improve the society in which we live. My friend's incident opened my eyes to the fact that we still struggle with many injustices. In America, though the situation for women is different than it is in Iran, it is not all *that* different. Although American women have more freedom than before, many minority groups as well as women are still relatively powerless. Same sex couples, for example, are often perceived as immoral and treated as outcasts. In order to be themselves and be happy, they surely do not have many options to pursue. How many others will find themselves faced with only painful options before society realizes that its beliefs, like the beliefs Edna faced, are outdated and causing immense suffering? I wish I knew a way to help people realize that each person's individuality and differences are not threats to society—that these differences can actually help us grow and be more productive! I guess if I knew the way to do that, I would bring world peace and much more, and become the most important person in history. Well, that is unlikely, but I hope there are some people out there who are brave enough to think and behave more fairly, and that as time passes these people grow in number to help make humanity more humane.

Supplemental Reading

Auden, W. H.: "Musee des Beaux Arts"
http://www.bu.edu/favoritepoem/poems/auden/musee.html

Bambara, Toni Cade: "The Lesson"
http://72.14.203.104/
search?q=cache:qt647fTso9oJ:home.olemiss.edu/~jmitchel/class/
bambara.htm+bambara+%22the+lesson%22&hl=en&gl=us&ct=clnk&cd=1

Barry, Dave: "Another Road Hog with To Much Oink"
http://www.miami.com/mld/miamiherald/living/columnists/
dave_barry/11073292.htm

Frost, Robert: "Mending Wall"
http://www.bartleby.com/118/2.html

Jackson, Shirley: "The Lottery"
http://www.classicshorts.com/stories/lotry.html

Plath, Sylvia: "Mushrooms"
http://www.poemhunter.com/p/m/
poem.asp?poet=6642&poem=33187

Vowell, Sarah: "Cowboys v. Mounties"
in *The Partly Cloudy Patriot*

Wright, James: "Small Frogs Killed on the Highway"
http://plagiarist.com/poetry/?wid=7153

Acknowledgments

"Sonnet for Carryhouse and Keeper," "How to Keep a Setter," "The Dark Pelican," "The San Simeon Zebras," and "Field Notes" are reprinted by permission of the author. "Who'll Say Dugong When the Dugong's Gone" is reprinted by permission of the author. "Plea for a Captive" is reprinted by permission of the author. "Coyotes" is reprinted by permission of the author. "The Climbers" is reprinted by permission of the author. "Peacock Display" is reprinted by permission of the author. "The Puppy" is reprinted by permission of the author. "Natural Enemies" and "West Nile" are reprinted by permission of the author. "Red & Black Days" and "Interlude: Still Sill" are reprinted by permission of the author. "September" is reprinted by permission of the author. "A Leopard Hanging in a Tree" is reprinted by permission of the author. "Pretty White Dress" is repritned by permission of Sarababande Books. "Sonnet" is reprinted by permission of the author. "Eurydice & Loverboy" is reprinted by permission of the author. "Echo & Narcicuss" is reprinted by permission of the author. "Mercy" is reprinted by permission of the author. "Song for a Mountain Climber" and "Ill-Made Almighty" are reprinted by permission of the author. "Laws of My Nature" and "Manifesto" are reprinted by permission of the author. "Hardware Sparrows" is reprinted by permission of the author. "Poppies" is reprinted by permission. "20 / 20" is reprinted by permission of the author. "Man Not Superman" is reprinted by permission of the author. "Orientation" is reprinted by permission of the author. "In Virgin Forest" from *Irons in the Fire* by John McPhee. Copyright (c) 1997 by John McPhee. Reprinted by permission of Farrar, Straus and Giroux, LLC. "The Giving Field" is reprinted by permission of the author. "Wake up People, Please!" is published here for the first time, with permission of the author.

Index of Authors

Index of Titles

Also available from Dream Horse Press:

Body Tapestries, S. D. Lishan

A Unified Theory of Light, Theodore Worozbyt

Baiting the Void, Penelope Scambly Schott

Wait for Me, I'm Gone, Amy Holman

Adam & Eve Go to the Zoo, Jason Gray

And We The Creatures, C. J. Sage, editor

New Fables, Old Songs, Rob Carney

Let's Not Sleep, C. J. Sage

The Florida Letters, Ryan G. Van Cleave

Situational Reality, Michael McNeilley

www.ingramcontent.com/pod-product-compliance
Lightning Source LLC
Chambersburg PA
CBHW031223090426
42740CB00007B/688